# We have a Jones for you

## Writers respond to the art of Fay Jones

Edited by Lou Rowan

Golden Handcuffs Review Publications
Seattle, Washington

# Golden Handcuffs Review
# Publications

A non-profit, traditional labor of love supported by readers, subscribers, donors, foundations, and tasteful advertisers.

Editor

*Lou Rowan*

Contributing Editors

*David Antin*
*Andrea Augé*
*Bernard Hœpffner*
*Stacey Levine*
*Harry Mathews*
*Rick Moody*
*Toby Olson*
*Jerome Rothenberg*
*Scott Thurston*
*Carol Watts*

LAYOUT MANAGEMENT BY PURE ENERGY PUBLISHING, SEATTLE
WWW.PUREENERGYPUB.COM

Libraries: *this is Volume II, #21.*

Information about subscriptions, donations, advertising at:
www.goldenhandcuffsreview.com

Or write to:   Editor, Golden Handcuffs Review Publications
1825 NE 58th Street, Seattle, WA 98105-2440

# Contents

NOTE: *The clearest reproductions of Fay Jones's drawings may be found on our website, www.goldenhandcuffsreview.com.*

*In many instances, the pieces refer to specific drawings. When this occurs, it is noted in parentheses at the end of the piece—except for one piece in which the number is part of the title.*

# Fay Jones
## drawings

1

MOVE BLUE

2

3

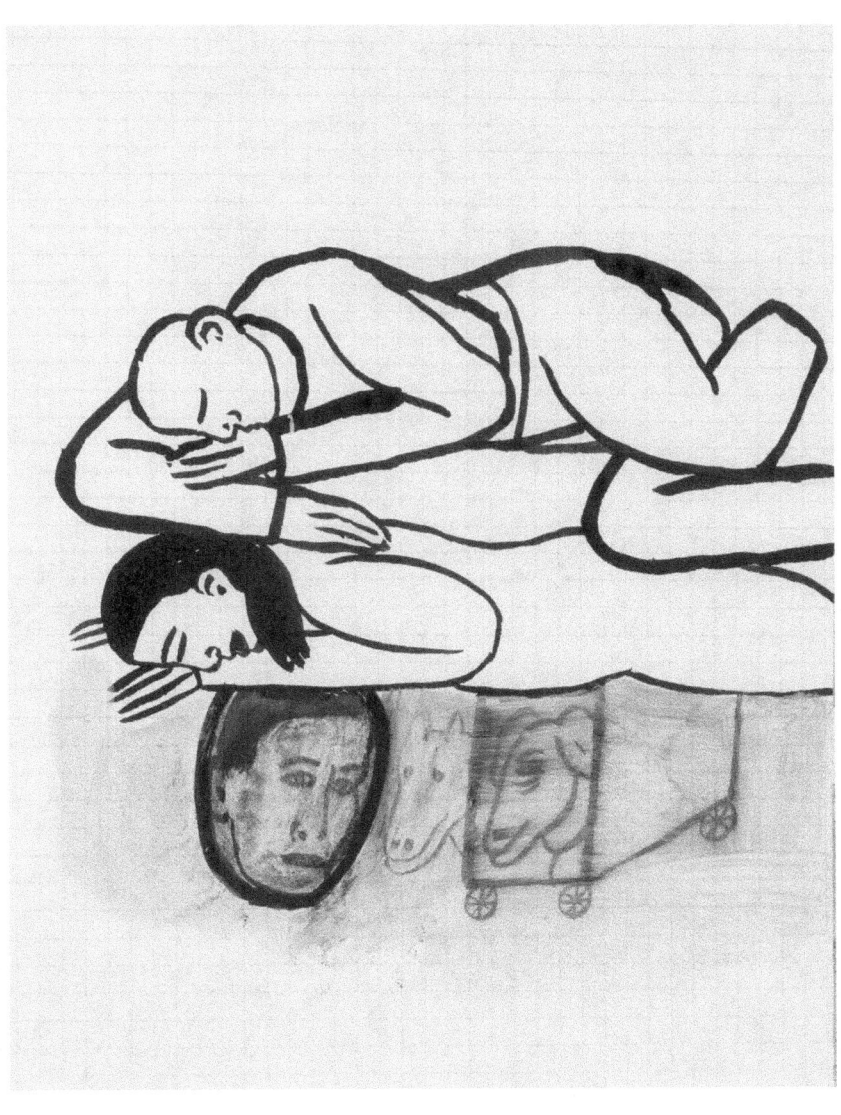

4

5

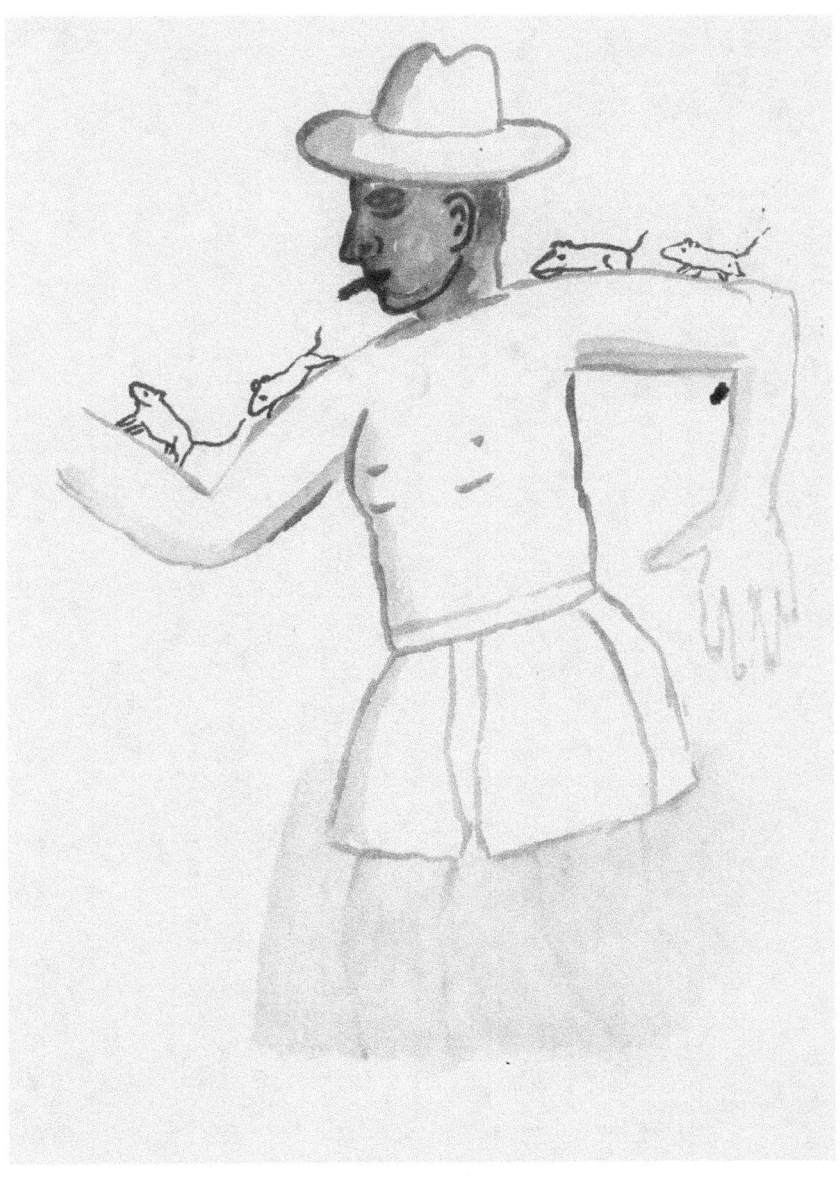

6

# Fay Jones

## *Rebecca Brown*

We went to see Fay Jones's studio. It's behind the house she shares with her husband, the painter Bob Jones. In the kitchen the cabinets are painted over with great big squares and circles and triangles of red, green, yellow, blue - the poster paint colors you'd find a child's toy box. Fay Jones painted them with her granddaughter. Why not. Fay Jones' paintings are sad and suggestive enough to appeal to story-seeking, melancholic me, but also bright and goofy funny enough to make a child laugh.

Bob Jones goes to work in his studio in the house; Fay Jones walks us out back to hers.

It's sunny and there's a porch and a canopy of fig trees and you walk down a staircase in dappling shade then down a couple more steps next to a garden. The building is tall, like a box on its side. There's a window up high, and on the walls the paintings and stuff she's working on. There's white rectangles framed by smudgy lines of paint where paintings in progress used to hang but have been taken down. They sort of remind me of windows except to where.

Fay Jones' work is full of characters who reappear: dancers and sailors and gamblers and swimmers and couples and men in hats. There are people who are part-person and part-something else: a rabbit and girl; a monkey and child; a woman and a mouse. They tell beast fables without the fable; they're tales without a moral or an end.

Chris and I went to Westlake Station to see the Fay Jones mural which is bigger than a bus, it's bigger than a train car. We stood on the platform opposite it and watched it in the gaps between the buses and trains that arrived and departed, we watched as parents and kids with suitcases and teenagers with backpacks and women and men with briefcases and bags schlepped on and off or rushed. On the mural above and behind them, like a great, big brightly colored thought bubble in a comic book, a couple danced, a man stood upright in a boat, and fish flew in the sky.

It's like the mural is glimpses of half-remembered daydreams of these travelers. Wherever they are, they're somewhere else. Whatever they want they almost see, although not ever quite. They might not be thinking directly of —- uh—- whatever. But something in them hovers. Whoever they're always imagining.

Do not ask what these pictures "mean". Don't try to make them tell you. Whatever does red or circle mean? Or shadow or rabbit or man. There is something balanced and something not in them. There is remembering longing and something that tells you look.

## FAY JONES dates*

1936: born, Boston.  Mother Hester Fay: hotelier, homemaker
Father Robeson Bailey; writer, faculty at Bread Loaf Writers
Conference, Smith, U of Oregon, etc.
Parents' friends include writers like Robert Frost, John Ciardi,
Dorothy Parker, etc.
1947: given a watercolor set
1953: begins study at RISD
1955: sees Mark Rothko exhibit: "It made me want to be myself."
1957: marries painter Robert (Bob) C. Jones
1958: gives birth to son, the first of four children
1960: moves to Seattle where Bob teaches art at UW
1970: first solo exhibit, Francine Seders Gallery
1980s: public art commission for Seattle Downtown Bus Tunnel
1996: Fay Jones: A 20 year Retrospective at Boise Art Museum
1997: Fay Jones: A 20 year Retrospective at Seattle Art Museum
2000: begins repainting Goya
2015: Golden Handcuffs Review issue devoted to Fay Jones

*With thanks to Sheila Farr, from whose book Fay Jones (University
of Washington Press, 2000) and essay on Jones at HistoryLink.org, I
got much of this information.*

# Blue Moves

## for and after Fay Jones

*Scott Thurston*

I thought in this universe
you could be my friend.
I am in ideas of the body,
a human standing in *wu-chi*
as the trapeze passes the constellation.

Gesture is how we mean in movement:
when I look out to sea
I feel the earwig climb my shoulder.
We provide the routes that animal forces traverse.

In our mangled desires
we lift out of ourselves:
tongues dart out like fishes,
two arms meld into one.

My science is not stable.

Why can we never balance
these aspects of our natures

before flying off the handle
into the dog's dinner?

My layers enfold
your dreams enfold
our layers meeting
the animal in my dream
and rolling it into yours.

Can we be bold and free, you and me?

# Man and Woman Reclining

## *Burt Kimmelman*

In our sleep we fold ourselves over
our dreams — to hold them, protect them. At
times I see you in my dream. Do you
see me too? They are there as we lie
over them — and we are there, dreaming
the same dream. No one else dreams our dream.

They are there and we are there too. Our
eyes are closed, and if we opened them
they would be gone. Would you be gone too?

(#3)

# The Siblings Jones

*Brian Marley*

Deep in Davy Jones's locker there's a scroll commemorating his late brother Casey, train wreck hero of popular renown. Davy, malevolent spirit of the seven seas, has borne many a shipwrecked sailor to a watery grave. But his behaviour is as nothing compared with Casey's satyrical philanderings, his monstrous drunken guilt, the way he whittled on the glans of his penis with a craft knife until, erect, it looked like an intricately carved mahoganny baluster, and in repose like a decaying vegetable. Had Casey been fired from his job on the Illinois Central Railroad, he could easily have joined the next freak show that passed through Water Valley. Of which Davy knew nothing. To this day he mourns the loss of his only brother.

But living in the ocean depths poses its own problems. Davy feels the cold more acutely than when he was a youngster, and over the years he's been obliged to shift his house nearer and nearer to a geothermal vent. The sulphurous stench used to bother him, but no more. Hot water streams constantly through the tightly meshed windows and doors and exits via cracks in the walls. His house badly needs caulking. Frankly, it needs a woman's touch. That's another thing Davy wouldn't know about.

Unless Casey's widow, Janie, gets her way, that is. She's

always been rather fond of Davy. The way she picked strands of dried sargassum out of his hair was noted by everyone, Casey included, which triggered another unhappy bout of philandering and whittling. She even claims to enjoy the company of Davy's boon companions: the swordfish, the giant squid, the great white shark, all of whom relish the human titbits he provides for them. Janie they give cold appraisal – is she food or not? Only time will tell.

No-one knows why Casey didn't leap to safety, why he held on to the brake lever after it was locked in position, after the engine was put in reverse, after the sanders were opened, and as the train slithered down the track towards catastrophe. The official report into the train wreck declined to speculate as to why Engineer Jones remained on the footplate. According to Davy, Casey was wrestling with the brake lever as with a laocoonian sea serpent. Or suchlike. Davy lives in a state of almost constant hallucination. But when reality is so strange, who can tell the difference?

The equinoctial tides are running high, higher than ever before. Towering waves are crashing together. Spray mists the face of the moon. Even in the ocean depths this turbulence can be felt. The water slews one way, then another, and during a particularly powerful surge Janie is swept off her feet and dumped, fishnet stockings and all, into Davy's lap. The nautical chart he was consulting sashays to the floor.

Janie and Davy, happily ensconced. Another storey has been added to the house. In the inky night (marginally inkier than the inky day), Davy works downstairs while Janie sleeps restlessly overhead, dreaming turbid dreams, her legs entwined in sheets of woven kelp. He's keen, as ever, to finish the task and join her in their bed of sponge and seaweed. But his concentration is shot. He's finding it hard to tally up, harder still to reconcile his joy with the sailors' last words, their pitiful cries and exclamations.

An architectural peculiarity of the house is a narrow staircase, an inch or two wide, up which Davy's pet eel, Casanova, slithers.

# 3 for Fay Jones

*Marthe Reed*

a fish *is* a tongue
an embrace gone missing

caught there
among weeds

splatters of love
blood

's matter
your eyes forget fish

even   small fry
red mouths

red tongues
red's hurt

hunger also wagging
touch has

its own vernacular
shiver and glide

a clearer deeper ground
underneath

net's fraught
pursuit

fingers   tongues   hips
throes of the dice

(#2)

improvisation: ant    aunt    ought
she bears a fish home from the market
though sky fails to forecast day
amenable as everything

carried through you
signaling neither fresh nor dear
later feet upon a stool
she looses her hair from its catch

ink displaces rain
working a crease
still the ant
and flowers uncut

a cat bathes in shade's
ferny reach
and light grazes her shoulder
possibly amnesiac

stung while weeding
summer's relentless wresting
one life from another
blue finds its blue core

three notes descending
blue ink
or black
a brute force projected

like a bruise
wingless females and queens
epithelial notations
ante    emete    ameise

auntie's sharp tongue
her shoulder also
sweat in wet runnels
down her breasts and back

insects busy in the earth
flowers and fishskin foraging

(cover)

time slips
outofhand

            or reckoning
                line

               takes its own direction
       the illusive nature of shadow

it might be
[im]possible to read the past
   near
        -ly

       not there
   naught to be seen          neither particle nor—

            figures a-march fore and
   aft the ground
    nothing is certain
       [[ *quantum sufficit*

the motion of time reduced to a wave

    super.
im position   *remember to—*
   counting backward toward insipience

   sleek lines and pointed toes
   [[ heel-to-toe heel-to-toe

           brownian motives
              motion

i have forgotten my lines
  left them

        lies lies   lies

    (#4)

# Like a Fish

*Philip Terry*

when I see
a fish I feel
like a fish
I feel like my tongue
is a fish or
like a fish
like the way
it moves
like a fish
in and
like a fish
out like
like a fish
trying to escape
like a fish
from a hole
in a like rock and
like a fish
something is
stopping it

from like leaving
like a hook
caught in its gills
like a fish
taut on a line
like a fish
and perhaps that's why
like a fish
I can see like blood
like a fish
on the rocks
and now
like a fish
my eyes
are like the
eyes of a fish
still and placid and
like a fish
not giving
like a fish
much like away
but definitely
like a fish
mournful when
you look closely
and then
like a fish
I start to think
what would I
like feel if
like a fish
someone
stuck a hook
in my like tongue
like a fish
and started
tugging it
like a fish
I'd think get the

like a fish
fuck off wouldn't I
I'd think take your
hook off of my tongue
like please
like a fish
you've no
business doing that
and then
like a fish
I'd think that
like a fish
if fish
could
like a fish
talk
like a fish
they'd say
that like too

(#2)

# Private View

texts in response to seven drawings by Fay Jones

## *Paul A. Green*

The poltroon cadets, powder-faced, have flattened their heads. Up against the wall, boys. Hover in your stuffy tunics, hang in a cone of weak grey radiance.  You have been installed to radiate potency but never on tip-toe over  such heaped vegetables. Those uniforms were acquired at the barrel of a gun.  You are now stateless. Spiked hounds, playing to the gallery, consume vegetables and/or rabbits. It's all been framed by quick quasi-geometrical work on the brushes, a wavering cube of contra-indications. The canines have been partially redacted. We are now artfully stateless.

(#1)

Those fish have all the right semiotics. The greater/lesser fishes of the catacombs in brilliant black on white. They are blotched with a fine array of sins, such a finny flock. Up in a shadow patch, a sin in progress even as I speak. The Right Man, a concept borrowed from A.E Van Vogt, spits on the other cheek to ensure dominance, as a victim 'presents tongue' to signify submission while focusing on a vanishing point, the  observer in retreat.

(#2)

Introducing the cult of the clenched fish. Keep it close to your heart, and keep talking. Customary to turn your back and turn the lights low as you are deftly processed into line-dancing. Shoulder the weight of the thick insect. It moves in stop-motion. The click of synchronised legs. Let me pull your hair if you need a warning signal. The exotic lure of the Orient in the lineage of those cheeks. Call me a patriarch if you dare.

(cover)

Sleeping for years. That's the hieroglyph I prefer. She's carrying a sac of woe, the babel-head who betrayed her but he's under wraps now. I could squeal with glee, once upon a time-machine. Now now, it's onward and inwards. A typical dog is boxed up, it's the only thing that keeps her suspended but even he's astral travelling, his double ganging up on her.

(#3)

The Headless One in motion. It is presenting as a ghost tripod, dragging a leg-over. The astral body has fermented. It's blotted its copycat. It is poised to fall on its feet and its face, not its arse. That tree is in a universe on the next block. The danger is contained by wet stripes.

(#4)

The hero rats are rolling along the neckline under the Conjurer's hypno glance. He keeps himself under his hat for shadowing. Nicotine Harry and his Rampant Rodents. A tail is his secret fuse. It's trickery with his pants smoked out. The music of the maestros blares forth. Everything in the zone of the showtime was conducted via his passive voice.

(#5)

Greetings from the flailing trapezes. Their heads are large but their limbs are small. Burt Lancaster filmed this in black and in white. The glaring young man. Trapezes cross the borders of states, all the roadmaps anchored so gravely on the news. They transcend the Sign of the Donkey, under which we will all die, trundling to Jerusalem. The Donkey is inverted, an adverse signifier.

(#6)

# Move Blue

*Lance Olsen*

The man in black begins sleeping on top of me again. He doesn't wear black, of course. He wears long grayish underwear and possesses no eyebrows. Breathing is difficult for me, but that might be a different story.

The man in black who doesn't wear black lacks a left foot. I don't know why. A train. A trap. A bomb. Sometimes these things happen. Sometimes they don't. For him walking is worry, a kind of continuous lopsided barging. I imagine. I mean, I wouldn't know. He always crawls on top of me after I'm already in bed, already asleep, face down. He wears a gold nose stud.

Before he crawls on top of me after I'm already in bed, already asleep, he removes his face, slips it into a large bowl of the sort in which you might house goldfish, and slides it beneath the bed, my bed, our bed, in a manner of speaking, at an angle that allows it, the face, to watch my room from the floorboards up to, roughly, about a yard off the ground.

He is bald and keeps his dog there, too: beneath my bed. In a clear-sided box on wheels. Because he—I think it is a he, the dog—has no legs. It is tubular, all head and torso, and missing an eye. This dog (what kind, I can't say) dreams (I imagine he dreams; I wouldn't know)—this dog dreams he is an alligator with two eyes, as dogs will do if they are of a certain size.

Breathing is difficult, as I say. Naturally. This is earth. This is gravity. And sometimes I wake up unable to move, the man in black who doesn't wear black has pinned me down so heavily, pressed my face into the mattress. My theory is he gains weight as his dreams. Or perhaps his dreams themselves gain weight, load him up with contingencies. This is Berlin. This is Seattle. Etc. We met online.

I want to say we met online. I want to say I recall such things. I want to say—I don't know why—the man in black who doesn't wear black messaged me on Facebook. Maybe he sent me a friend request. Maybe I accepted. Maybe I always accept friend requests. Maybe whether or not I know the person who sent them. I want to say this makes me feel like I have friends, maybe.

His message urged me not to be afraid. He wasn't crazy or anything, it said. He simply had a crush on me. A long-distance crush. He wouldn't bother me again if I didn't want him to bother me again. All I had to do was tell him to go away. He just wanted me to know.

I didn't respond. He messaged me again. I didn't respond again. He messaged me again. I responded. I can't let messages go un-responded to. This is who I am. It feels like an untidy bathroom inside my head. It feels like ingurgitated trunks in small cars.

This went on for a while and then I blocked him and fell asleep and sometime during the night when all the colors go away I felt him drag himself up on top of me. I conjecture he climbed in through my apartment window, my first-floor apartment window, and there was absolutely nothing sexual between us: just his weight, his face, his dog, his friend request. Etc.

I sleep on my stomach, mostly, having a bad back, needing to stretch out my vertebrae nocturnally.

His weight, his face, his dog, his friend request, his lack of eyebrows and foot, his breath (a combination of lemons and cat shit), and sometimes I'd awaken, moonlight fluorescing colorlessly, to find him whispering into my ear, all seashell hiss.

*Move blue*, he'd ocean at me. *Move blue.*

Sometimes I'd awaken to find my hand feeling his face in the fishbowl beneath our bed. It, my hand, had a mind of its own. My hand was its own person. The man in black etc. let me investigate bumps, nodes, flaps, inconsistencies, pinprick stubble, warm eyeballs drier than you might assume. They didn't blink, the eyeballs, just swiveled in my direction, lidless.

Sometimes I awaken to my forefinger sliding around inside his black-lipped mouth.

The rest of his skin is a shade of grammar-school paste.

The tongue. The heat. The broken teeth.

Every morning when I revive the man in black etc., his face in the fishbowl, and his dreaming dog in the clear-sided box are gone.

I never hear him pack. I never hear them leave.

By the time I shut off the shower I can barely remember he's visited. This is brain matter. This is abstract thought contained in 1130 cubic centimeters with the consistency of soft gelatin.

*Move blue. Move blue.*

By the time I dress and bus or bike or subway (I don't recall which) to my job two floors below street level translating strangers' prose into a language that doesn't hurt, much, I've stopped shaking, because I've forgotten he'll return every night, except sometimes he won't, he has a life of his own, and on weekends I wander through the loud, compressed stalls at the farmers market or sip coffee in a loud, compressed café down the street while reading the loud, compressed news on my iPad.

This goes on for a while and he lets me run my thumb over his shattered lower cuspids and lower lateral and central incisors, love him free and clear, except that I don't, except that I do. Etc.

Breathing is difficult and other things might have happened, needless to say. Birds, for instance. There could have been a flock of black smiles ascending. Unexpected proportions. (There are always unexpected proportions, are there not?) And at one point in my life I could have lived in Barbados, is the point. At another I could have written screenplays involving detectives and low-key black-and-white visuals. I have always been a fan of German cinema.

He could have left for good, the man in black etc., but he didn't, doesn't. He could have stayed for good, but he didn't, doesn't. I could have further forgotten about him. I could have cared about him.

There could have been more activity in my cerebral cortex, less hope, more whiskey, another zombie movie, someone's oily gun, another round of electroconvulsive therapy, someone else's belief in the empowerment of yoga or identity politics or bite guards or mathematical clarity or pupillary light reflexes.

But that would have been a different story. Those would have been different stories. This one isn't like those at all. This one is precisely like those in every way. This one just stops when you least expect it.

(#3)

# The Aselline Starlets

*Peter Hughes*

I

I said this imagery
was mental but
she claimed you
can't say what's
happening within
a composition
as the flicks & swerves
are too precise &
fast to verbalize
& also donkeys
are usually top heavy
as well as too
heavy to catch when
suspended from your
thoughts & old arcs
carry memories
of awkward turns
& ecstasy
each thought is made

of temporary nodes
we sometimes fresco
on the ceiling
but usually do not
because you know
death intervenes
or we get banished
from our provinces
by the council or the
gravities of love
& cooking then learning
this new scale or
trying to catch a flatfish
or anticipating flight
again become
the medium in which
these things happen
but we nearly know
it's impossible except in
certain kinds of art
to fly forever


II


we try to fly
above the heads
of propaganda
we partner novel forces
& the fatal graphs
of lost momentum
the show's constructed
on a person's wrist
sweaty & chaffing
lost in lights
made up
accommodating
glitter falling
balancing above
a couple of tunes

III

all the goodness
sucked out of the
neighbours & bound
to a stick with
mallarky & duct tape
was what they opted
to salute & strive for
songs of old rope
& sail-cloth embellished
with the sooty mould
of who gives a shit
we proceeded to erect
this monument to
the history of art
about camping & sex
with crumbs & mildew
where the nearest
place for milk was Wales
it's as if you go back
to an old town that's
dead in you forever
each time you open
your mouth to speak
& no speech comes

IV

we dreamt there'd
been a rupture
in the weather
& we were entering
Steve Swallow's
disco period sideways
late into the night
I read the tattoo'd lady
without really
taking it in

the waste-ground
wind is whispering
we each have
decomposing caravans
parked inside our heads
rats' droppings
sketches &
rubber jewels
wait for the moon
to make the first move


V


no-one came from
miles around these fields
of moonlit pumpkin
the substitute ring-
meister can't decide
whether to dance in
bed to Chopin or lean
out of the flap to see
if it's the bailiffs
one of the flying goats
is off on an away day
to express this
play any note
well not that one
a semitone higher
or lower
& nod


VI


I'm no longer
with the circus
except sometimes
briefly in the memory
of strangers
I reached a point

where all I saw
were messages
from Mary
cross-stitched on
those overarching
canvas skies
still I do do the same
route at the same times
sleep in the car
register the music
now & then
with the window down
when the wind is right
but we don't interact
the time for such things
closed its eyes & rolled
back under the waves
they never see me park
or circle the compound
or swoop overhead

(#6)

# If Our Garden Is But a Pot of Wandering Sailor

*Sarah Mangold*

Hart to commemorate the name
All among the fruit trees
The rather ripe cherry trees
One little pear tree
For one apple quince tree
For flowers called anemone
For sixteen province roses
For one great cherry
For one dozen black currants
Cherries of the long speckled
Cherries of the last ripe
Pears of Gratiola
Pears the porting all
And one butterfly resembling
A perfect bird
The Roman peach
The dapper plum of Malta

(#1)

# Membrane

### Fay Jones, 1936 -

## *Jed Myers*

There are the iconic particulars in both
worlds, either side of the portal—

hats are big, brimmed portable
shadows; dresses advertise

nakedness; newborns, assuming
nothing, hover over us weightless;

dark waterbirds are the thoughts
no one owns.... Both worlds,

both theaters of chance, are filled
with unconsciousness, like fish in the air

where we swim, hands useless
beyond a few cards and sensations. Each

thing whether here or there houses
its cache of perplexed desire. Each

eye is a speechless question, mouth
a silently silenced cry, outreaching

arm a bridge our blindnesses itch
to cross. In both atmospheres, aimless

creatures watch like mute commentators
on all the unfinished he-and-she plots.

Who dies? That's nobody's business.
Not even she, the artist, can stop

the burning of secrets, the blanking
out of the flares of need, the unnoticed

disappearance of horizons, no matter
how accurate her depictions might be

for both universes on that one window
they share. And not even she can think,

paint, draw, nor dream her way through
to the other side of the screen. (From either,

one might peer into the other, but never
one's own.) Not even she

who attends the membrane between
stands a chance of crossing to look

back, into this our unknowing
clay—back, in through the manifold

densities of our dark wings, gray
hats, pale shoulders and their galactic-black

insect trespassers—to witness
what here is invisible, the coursing

inside of our dreads and hopes. So she keeps
reaching, as if her hand could stretch

the dimensionless skin of that magic
rectangle, as if she could capture

the contours of the flesh of that world's
captives as they happen to pass

close, as if her finger might brush
the lashes of those thin slits under

their safe-house brows, or graze those lips
closed on their smoking tongues, as if

by such devotion to otherness,
what's in us after all could be known.

She lifts her tapered implements, traces
those denizens' beautiful lostness—

as if by this we'll sense our own.

# Five for Fay Jones

*Jeff Hilson*

i
O little fan I wouldn't start but start. "Hoo hoo" to the owl (thou, o
owl). His reply: "You are half-a-fish, head and back, and mute. I am
a dish here. Only my silver threads is coming on. They do so. I am
afraid of the bones of fish." His reply: "O jones." His reply: "That I run
with a shell through the streets." His reply: "weep weep." His reply:
"Look how I am the same as pussy." His reply: "This went on for
hours, and on the wing too." Broken he is see a round talker, all feint,
drawing you off. Give him the shakes, ask him about the leads, about
there, the shakes. He never heard our conference.

ii
Who love's to catch a grayling. At any rate them or gold head hares.
What a day. Tap tap tap the nymphs are bumping the whole team of
nymphs. So I have to change my rig & dee knows this dee & dove
because their all still flies. Anyway tug tug tug I touch the nymph like
any secret watcher & it began to hurt right up to the whip-finish. But
the grayling holds. But also the best beats lie hanging over in the
breeze & quaking. So another rise lifting to a small brown up-wing.
Then I wonder at the bank-side if their on the move. Maybe their

getting ready to move to test out where the best beats lie? Anyhow only one more hook one fingerling & I slip off I'm base I'm scarce I'm silvery all over.

iii

I was looking 'channel-ish,' edgy comme, a bit overboard in the dowdy channel. All the day-boats burning, I described the sea as good as bill this time the poet bill. The sea described below. I hate poissons. I'm glad the fishery crashed. But I'd like to tell you about my bird. He's running back to reculver. How to get there: there's an oar farm there's an eel rack. Be confused. Clubrush in the fleets and rhines. In any case the blue wave is moving to the right. There is error then and the orioles have moved it over. The hell I am. Hi ed hi lisa. I think I'll call my bird yvonne.

iv

Such trees as ships at sea. Still and slow the voyage of the briar. To time in swims as much yellow as a bell singing, "my holly smells of fish which one the rarest one my letters plain" (song xxv). Clanging with the hens this useless bird is out. There was ruffs and reeves, and velvet runners, and there was swans. It fell in the ouse with ribbons. Look there are more behind. Their names are claire and julie and they too dream of being on thorns. A whistle for each as they fall in and change. Such trees as when the flowers appear before the leaves. I make it up again. The flowers they sell best at sea. Listen…

v

Found out late $n = 2$ and that the wind does this to all numbers so as $n$ approaches and $p$ approaches $np$ approaches. I love $n$ more than $p$. It's in poissons as I said before & in the blind probably. $N$ hunters. The d-ducks are d-dead after the $n$ hunters shoot. Hunters with lovely famous cash probably. And in the pond that is the decoy pond in other words I stole it from your head of creative writing that my heart melts in me. And in the lane a leaf is on what I love, or none. The shiny round alternatives birds need. Facing into the wind, successful in the blind, the old hunter he is the one at wrotham at fritton and at ranworth.

# Host this

*Carol Watts*

Something crawls up
unawares
let it not be picked off by birds
or mistake me
for a walnut tree
while I wonder
which is host here
ah   it is
you

                        (cover)

Promise me
speech
for as long as it takes
to mend
all this
*la lengua en la mano*
here they predict
the earth's ending

in scales
that mythic catch
flapping &
tired
always beginning
& there
again

                (#2)


So many years
in parallel
I get real rest in
hospitality
dreams
the ones
that take on
full & caged
menageries
I spent
nights
cradling them
quiet
but try
barking at dawn
now I've reached
my 50s
along with
all the
others

                (#3)


See
the capacity
for song
in the darkest times
even mice
sing as they roam

'somewhere between
the sound of birdsong
& clean glass
being scrubbed'
the more complex
the more absent
she
may be testing
his memory for
songspiel
shouldered
outside
the usual
range

(#4)


What it was
to find joy
leaping over
labour
work doesn't lie
in docile nets
while life flick-flacks
or soars
catch me you say?
these days
work is a circus
its own abandon
driven
over time's duller burdens
& lenticular limbs
like living
leap here!
catch!

(#5)

# *3 after* Fay Jones

## *Judith Skillman*

The insect climbs my back
while I carry the fish.
I feel black legs walking.

The gills I imagine
to be translucent flaps
squeak as I walk.

In this fog of gesso
a beetle mimics
the strap of my dress.

Alack, a gritty flesh
comes between my longing
and what I have lost.

Here is the just-caught fish,
a mermaid's tail
in the wrong place.

You see the rain and sense
a face turned away,
a dark eye.

A few drops fall
before fallow times.
How large the insoluble.

The pose held by the grip
of bent antennae
to forge such a slender waist.

And why the nape?
Can a bare shoulder
ever imitate a breast?

(cover)


*(2 after #2)*

Lick me, I said, and I will lick you.

We will fish below the surface for the Cubans.

Perhaps the milfoil will take us captive.

Let our tongues flatten.

Let's quit drowning, and go instead towards diagonals.

There must be two of us.

You remain apart despite the nose.

I am tired of bereavement.

We are only mimes who cry when they pull our strings.

Wait, you have a bit of fish tail in your ear.

I'll wipe it from the board while you write those theoretical equations.

I'll salivate for you to prove it's a science.

Hunger for answers.

The stars shine more brightly in the southern hemisphere.

I have tried the shark of grief.

Still we have no teeth with which to dismiss attachment.

It's just the two of us outlasting the big cats.

Don't be so heavy-lidded.

Addle me you fishy whore.

************

Perhaps the slime of this will make us both smart and salty. Let our tongues lose their words, and gather the glitter of worn out time. Let's quit before we grow any farther down. The flat world, the drowning. Let's leave the obvious and go where the head remains attached to its body, for there must be two of everything. I am tired of the way they talk about bereavement. As if it had a head and a body, when the birds refuse to sing. We are only mimes who talk when they pull our strings. Oh you have a bit of fish tail in your ear. Here, I will wipe it from the white board. Then we'll continue with theoretical ponderings, equations, and the dim stars below us may shine more brightly in the southern hemisphere. For I have tried the shark of grief. Face it. Genderless or female, we outlasted the big cats and all that shone rabbit-eyed. Give me your tongue, that plank of sod painted mars red in the bright-dark.

# 4 Poems

*Terry Martin*

**Brief Encounter with Anxiety**

*Let me be your carnival ride*
the pale man tells the mice,
lighting a cigarette, closing
his eyes, assuming the pose.
Doubts and worries, niggling regrets,
shadowy fears scamper and skittle
across his shoulders, down his arms.
When one jumps off, another joins
the endless conga line. Noses
twitch along, whiskers tickling.
Centered by his brown felt hat,
the man sways his torso,
first to one side, then the other,
tilting to tinny circus music.
*No hurry, no worry* he assures
the rodents. *I can go on like this
for days.* Nothing on their minds
but the cube of cheese waiting

at the end of the maze of him.
On and on they scurry,
carefully avoiding
the glowing orange tip.

(#5)

## And Apricots

After Praxilla of Sicyon
Greece, 450 B.C.

Loveliest of what I'll leave behind
        is the desert night sky
and loveliest after that Jane's knowing eyes
        and the river's song
then there's summer tomatoes
        with mozzarella and basil
three friends I've kept longest
        the dog's ecstatic greeting
but also Stafford's poems
        breath keeping the pulse
steady in my wrist Sting's "Fields of Gold"
        waking to a rooster's crow
and apricots ripening on our tree

(#6)

## No Partner Today, Only the Beat of His Crazed Heart

Shuffle 1-2-3, shuffle 1-2-3
Doin' a silent cha cha cha
Shuffle 1-2-3, shuffle 1-2-3
Movin' to the cosmic sis-boom-bah
One foot in front of the other
That's all he's got to do
Findin' the steps he needs
Dancin' his own way through.

(#4)

## Water Signs

Her mother is a bone
       caught in her throat.
Her father searches
       for the bliss of shadow
in extreme heat.
       She carries them both.
              (cover)

# 7 Poems

*Jim Goar*

On fields of graph paper and you beside
me. Dreamt. These dogs
oh boxes silent. Who so bold as hair by
boldest hair? I claim
vanity mirrors heads with hearing.
Listing hands so redacted up
my sleeve for you and only you. In boxes.
Calligraphy for thou is serifa font.

(#3)

***

saddle my donkey
      at folklore eyes almost touching.  I've stretched    to me
  though you   in mirror.    I will    not go    falling
    to the next        shapes without
 depth. A leash
        We flip. Our eggs. The young
    pearls of hazing. Do not question    a shark on bended
knee.

(#6)

***

A likely story                    pools over. Evidence
                    suggests the fish
        dresses squarely shouldered.        Each line meets its marker in
            hushed judicial tones. This began as a mermaid dressed
                        as Marco Pollo.
                        (cover)

\*\*\*


While sea toy soldiers.
While rabbits inevitably blue.
While garlands farewell competing face.
While perspective blankets pirate skies.
While flotsam hackneys sleeping hound.
                        (#1)

\*\*\*


Fish fall into perfectly bound motion. Tongues a twitter
while gills floss the night.   These are symbols
reminding of perspective. Those damn prints
across the page where faces used to see. Surfboards
wax poetic while lipstick eyes roll on.
                        (#2)

\*\*\*


Should we assume the mice run right to left? And you, who read this,
left to right. We await translation. Indenting the deepest night. From
the farthest east. I'm not sure what to tell you. There used to be a
box.
Its shadow. Tells us of the sun.
                        (#5)

\*\*\*


There is an octopus inside  penis. These men with their
                        heads in the
                        clouds. I guess. This is when we call to
those who are listing.
                        (#4)

# Four Ekphrastic Poems for Fay Jones

*Andrew Mossin*

I

The tongue was a lair of sound
bred from black night.

The tongue was participant
in the rites of memory bled from deformed alphabets.

The tongue was absolute mistress
absolute master awake in their synthesis of coral and reed.

The tongue was a zone of offering
a radical smith hammering its name into the dust.

The tongue was care-giver
mother of mouthings awake in dark branches of olive.

The tongue bore withdrawn thirst of the scorpion
an imploded moon incised on its thrice-cut cheek.

The tongue like a black wing slit at its root
roaming the molecular sheen of its bloodsoaked tendon.

The tongue like lozenges of manna.  Spoors of silica and jasmine.
Celibate stone's black octagon of vapor and cloud.

The tongue deserted inside a frame of coronal dusk.
Black on black where palm inserted itself into optic sea's
            phosphorescent glow.

The tongue inebriated below zero from the guano islands
descending from ledges of coral blood and olive.

Brittle triadic beat of its incantatory mutter.
Neutered tongue's nomadic spirit braided from seraphic scrawl.

The tongue blazing inside an illiterate's mercurial knot
wings of its speech caught in a stream of epigonic loss.

The tongue's declivity held by palm's woeful prophecy.
Mollusk and crab silenced in paroxysms of light and shadow.

Tongue's blackened fin nearing the water's edge.

(#2)

II

> *At night onto its branches come*
> *the souls of ancient birds.*
>            Federico García Lorca

To remember what they stored away what they gave....

Incipient cycle immersed in its eidetic movement.  'There was a time'
Orphic regression says and releases it again in the time of its saying.
        A body

unclothed by what it meant to say, a body blackened by the body of
        another
black and white bodies inside the principle movement of their
        sounding.

There is sunlight where the recumbent figure is itself a skinned
palm released inside a circle of light, diaphanous

refugeed beings stranded in the queer sun, stained as if to be seen
were a version of sight formed from black ocean's mineral.

An intaglio brought back in glimpses, black lines
revealing the space between hand and torso

each space in which the other rests unannounced
like a lattice of stars drawn over ligatures

where the heavens once parted.  Their horizontal coil
laid end to end like a ring of perdition, a host of animated silence.

Neutered in their mesmeric sphere, they sing without
voice cloaked in the alembic vertigo of insinuated motion.

Night's forecast bled from each ruptured thigh.
Birds of ever after singing through black boxes of rain and wind.

What condemns their psychic draft to this ward
without stars, ambient regressions of tone scarred by monsoons of
      ancient rain

similar to the laired resistance of coral
held in combustive assonances of phrasal geography?

Zodiacal light stripped from their bodies
leaving them in positions of abject migration

blazing atop cylindrical beams lettered in fugitive script
deposited at eye level underneath horizons of mnemonic loss

captive's scree striated by sunlight's horizontal strips
animated against their will by ecliptic feral routes

movement's reliquary light suspended on cargoes of canine ferocity.

(#3)

III

"But when with vows
      and prayers I
appealed to them, I took
the sheep and slit their throats
I ate by the water's edge I drank
blood from the trough of angels
sat near the sea of embers—

Dark blood flowed.  From out of Erebos
came gathering the spirits of the dead.
I unhoused myself I drew from the gathering
spirits I bathed in blood's crown
And saw the new brides and unmarried youths and
      toil-work old men
And those pierced by bronze-
tipped spears and those killed in battle
I saw them on the ground in their armor
stained with blood.  And I listened
for their voices near the sea and saw their
bodies in a trough of blood and I prayed
for deliverance from them
and one I did not know

      sat in conversation with them
      and steadied himself near their silent forms:

'Hear me, O rivers,' he said, 'hear me punished
by those who are done with life, hear me
cry out from the trough of blood, I have come
back to land, I have come to ask how to reach the land
of Telemachus, my own son whom I left in a nurse's
arms, I left my own son in a nurse's arms, I have come
back to ask how to reach land.'

And I sat with him
where blood flowed from the trough
his vows and prayers like my own passed

over the tribes of the dead, his hands like my own
blood-covered, his shield stained.  He said
he had come to reach land of the dead, he had come
to ask how to reach land of the dead.

Standing beside him I
          cried these words.  I entered
     the trough of blood alone I stood
                where he no longer stood.

And I remembered Circe's counsels....who knew
all the poisons which the broad earth grows.
And I saw the distant wave of Acheron
as if there were two winds passing over us
and one fought with lions and the other with Cocytus and Lethe
while its body blued out over sea's rough wave
a passing stranger like my own self
come to rest beside  me.

And when I lay down with him the sun was high in the heavens
          And Stranger stood round the trough and stared
                into the heavens and lay himself
          down among the dead his body near
                death worked its way forward to reveal black ribs
                    of a fishtail scarred and whitening

     pale in the noonday sun."

                    (cover)

IV

Stranger passes in his movement estranged by what he cannot be.
Stranger in his passing moving estranged from what he cannot
        become.

The voice of stranger when he rises like columella of a bird of death.
The voice of stranger when he wakes beside the bird of death.

There is waking there is the aftermath of waking when he wakes and
        sees where he has gone.
There is waking there is the absence of waking he wakes to see where
        he has gone.

The body of stranger is a reflection of movement when he walks
        there is ground there is sky.
The body of stranger reflects what he saw when he wandered away
        from ground and sky.

Stranger without head in his eyes he has no head he is walking
        straight into the sea.
Stranger without eyes or head waking inside a dream of the bird of
        death.

The circle that is part of his body's movement as he walks into the
        sea.
The light that forms a circle in place of his body a bow of light
        blackening across the sea.

'Stranger where are you going inside the circle of light inside a body
        of light and water?
Stranger where are you going inside a circle of light and water?'

Stranger when he appears on the horizon a figure passing over earth
        and water.
Stranger when he appears no horizon can hide him no light can
        shadow his passing.

Strange to come back to him to enunciate his *dualitude* to exact his
    pain anew.
Strange to hear him come back from his *dualitude* experiencing his
    pain anew.

'Stranger a mouth of heaven is speaking a mouth of heaven and
    earth is speaking.
Stranger you are dark in heavens sky your mouth is dark in heavens
    sky.'

Pale sound he requires to live by himself stranger inside a circle of
    light.
Pale intricate sound he attends to night and day inside his circle of
    flight.

The heavens are passing stranger the heavens are passing overhead
    in a circle.

'Stranger where are you going?'

The heavens stranger…

(#4)

*29 June-13 July 2015*

Notes
cover: The source text for this poem is *The Greek Magical Papyri in Translation* (tr.
Hans Dieter Betz).
#4: The word "columella" appears in Will Alexander's *The Sri Lankan Loxodrome*,
where it is defined as "a rod in the middle ear of birds and reptiles, which functions
like the chain of bones in the human ear, conducting sound waves from the drum to
the inner ear" (101). The term "dualitude" is drawn from Henry Corbin's *Avicenna
and the Visionary Recital*, where it appears in the following context: "The soul
discovers itself to be the earthly counterpart of another being with which it forms a
totality that is dual in structure. The two elements of this *dualitude* may be called
the ego and the Self, or the transcendent celestial self and the earthly Self, or by still
other names" (20).

# Living Rooms of Strangers

*Breka Blakeslee*

There is always rain and the dog always barks. Except when there is snow and the dog is dead. But mostly: rain and barking. You wear the same sweater. It smells like the dog dead in the snow but you refuse to wash it because you say it smells like your grandmother. I am worried about your grandmother.

There's another falling star, you say.

It isn't normal to see stars falling in the rain but it always rains and stars need to fall. The dog is barking which means it is alive which means it is raining not snowing and we are watching stars fall.

You could wear a different sweater, she says.
I like it better when it snows, you say.
You could at least wash it, she says.

I want to say that I don't care what sweater you wear or how many times you wash it. That I hope your grandmother is okay. That I know she means a lot to you. But I don't.

She thinks the stars look like silver spears. You always argue with her.
No, you say, they look like shattered glass.

I am never there to hear the argument but I know it by heart. It begins with the visual aspect of things but moves into the artistic and then semantic and then philosophical and verges on religious and ends on the personal. Neither of you will change your opinion. I do not think you even listen to each other, but you think you listen to each other — I can tell.

You lie on the pavement worn out by the argument and the dog's barking and I pretend I can feel your heartbeat between everything that separates us. This pavement, for example. These walls. Space, and also time.

These things are constant, are always:
You always wear the same sweater.
It always rains.
You always argue with her and she never agrees with you.
The dog always barks — unless it is dead and there is snow.

Some nights there is no rain or stars or snow or dog. On those nights there is only you and her and me. We are inside. The room is small and there is no door. The windows look into the living rooms of strangers and those windows look into the living rooms of other strangers and those windows look into the living rooms of other strangers until there is a distant window with just the glimpse of rain or stars or snow if the dog is dead.

I am there and you are there and she is there. Neither of you will look at me. Silver spears she will whisper and you will say shattered glass and I will look into the lives of strangers and ignore the pressure of your bodies.

In one living room, there is a family playing Life like they are in a commercial. There is a smiling blond mother and a smiling brunette father and a smiling sandy haired boy and a smiling curly haired girl. The boy pulls a card that says he is getting married. He puts the pink plastic peg into his green plastic car next to the blue plastic peg. Nobody is having any fun.

I want to tell you about the past, about the time I worked as a magician's assistant and was cut in two. I was the head and she was the legs. Or it might have been that you were the legs or maybe it was someone we've never met. There was also an umbrella and coming in out of the rain. And the dog shaking water or crouched low and growling.

In another living room there is a couple pretending to argue. When they run out of accusations they pull pictures off the walls and out of photo albums. They pile them in the center of the room. When the pile is as large as a small child they set it on fire. They are having an excellent time.

I want to tell you about our history. How we met in the town where your grandmother lives and we brought flowers to her house at the end of the cul-de-sac in your old neighborhood. Or maybe we brought flowers to her grave at the end of the cul-de-sac in the memorial park. And there was a coffee shop and she was there. Or maybe it was a bar and I was drunk. But either way it was her and this was before you had that sweater and before this darkness. But I think maybe there was rain. And the dog hiding in its crate in the hall.

In another living room there is my family when I was a child. Or maybe it is a family that is identical to mine. The children sit in a row on the couch. The father sits in a recliner. The mother sits in a rocking chair. They are all eating takeout and they are all watching the television. The television is not turned on.

I want to tell you about before that. About before her. When it was just you and I and the sky like broken glass. You said the pavement was boring and I said the sky was frightening and so we only looked at each other but that was frightening too. And the snow was cold but not as wet as rain. You were wearing a different sweater and it smelt like the aftershave my father wore. And maybe we were standing in the atrium of the mall waiting for the rain to pass but I think it was a bus shelter and we couldn't recognize any of the constellations.

In another living room there is a child putting toys into the fish tank. Some float and some  sink. The water is getting closer to the top of the tank. The child puts toys into the tank until there are no toys left. Then the child scoops the fish out of the tank and throws them into the toy bin. The fish flop around. Their gills are very red. They open and close their mouths.

I want to tell you about the time I was locked inside a room with no way out. I pounded on the walls and shouted until my throat was sore but all I could hear was the dog barking. Then it stopped and the snow began. Or no actually, I think you finally came and told me I was drunk, and that there really was a door. Or maybe no, there was no door but I was dreaming and you woke me. But either way my throat was sore and I couldn't say, Thank you. Or, I was afraid. Or, I missed you.

In another living room there are two girls on a couch. One of them is masturbating. They are both bored.

I want to tell you about her and how she is the wrong shape for your torso how your legs don't match how there is enough space between your chests that you could lose things.

In another living room there is someone lying on the floor and watching the ceiling fan spinning faster and faster and faster until it is only a blur.

I want to tell you about the way the darkness closed in one morning when I was pouring cereal into a bowl.

In another living room there is nothing.

I want to tell you how not to lose things. I want to tell you about the magician. About the umbrella. About your grandmother's grave and the bus shelter and the cereal and the dog crate in the hall. And there was us and stillness and snow and not so much between us. For example, this darkness. The dog. Your sweater. The way she doesn't fit against your body. But it is raining now.

From a stranger's living room the dog barks. The lights go out in the rooms around us one by one, darkness moving outward window pane by window pane by window pane. The click of a light switch turning off, receding living room by living room by living room until all I can see is darkness. I cannot see you or her or stars or rain or snow. I cannot see the spaces where you don't fit around her. I cannot see the sweater you always wear. The dog is very close.

(#3)

# The Twins

## *Rebecca Brown*

They were Siamese twins connected at the something.  They couldn't move, I mean, apart.  They had to do always the same almost.

There was something between them.

They were like bellboys like bellhops like ticket-takers like the red-capped flying monkeys in *The Wizard of Oz* movie only human and blue.  They had busy hands though you can't see them being that way because they're quiet now.  There is so much one cannot see!

They were blue bellboys with a Prussian or bishop's hat or conehead or someone turned away from them behind them between them.  Could anyone not be aware of this?  There is so much one will not see.

They were with one another all the time.  They were so much alike it was like they had the same brain or could read each other's minds like back in the caveman days.  It's the way we used to communicate before language.  It could have been awesome to read each other's minds but also not sometimes, like the minds of people who seemed boring but you knew there had to be more of them but then you found out there is nothing, truly nothing going on in them, they really are just boring. Or someone heard you thinking things you were ashamed of or embarrassed by like how much you think about him and things that you want to do to him or how he doesn't think of you like that or actually even think of you at all. It might have been nice to learn those things and save time. But it might have been better not to hear what someone was thinking when it would take away your hope.

We must not call them Siamese anymore. That's racist. Plus, there isn't Siam anymore: it's Thailand. Plus, they aren't all from there although the most famous were, Chang and Eng. Chang and Eng married. Not each other but women. They each had kids with their respective wife, eleven and ten, respectively, per wife. The proper term nowadays is "co-joined."

There had to be two of everything though not exactly alike because we each should be our own independent person. But not so different as to incite envy though who can banish envy? Sometimes it's worse the more you are. Especially when one is becoming less and one is becoming more. Then one becomes boring and clingy and one becomes mean and annoyed and who can banish that? No-one. Not even if one is so full of love, so dumb with love, and one tries to be everything do everything give everything, all of oneself including what one is not. Then the other feels, Enough already, Give me some goddamned room! But if one is attached to one, then even if there is something between them whether Prussian bishop conehead negative space or nothing, one cannot give the room one wants despite how one might want. One cannot make you love me like you did.

Their little dogs knew them. Their dogs knew what's between them.
        The dogs were digging gnawing. They gnawed and
pawed and lay something at their feet. Not slippers, not the paper, something limp. If you picked it up you would wish you hadn't.
        The dogs were white, the boys were blue.
        The boys were sad.

Their hats were like if a Guardia Civil hat and a flying monkey hat from *The Wizard of Oz* had a baby.  The backs of hats of the Guardia Civil were flat from when they had been pressed to the wall in the Civil War.  After they won they were heroes to almost everyone, though secretly hated by everyone else.  Then after they lost they were hated not secretly by almost everyone.  You never knew who was who because people change.

It wasn't dramatic like brother against brother, father against son (*nota bene* the absence of females in all these comparisons).  Had they been smashed against something too?  They stood on their tip-toes like sneaking.  They were holding their breath or breaths like, Get this over with! Or like, Don't let this ever end! Please God, let it remain like this forever! So loving and so close! So twinned! So close and in so love so what I have been wanting all my life so I can almost touch you now, your back, your hair--
     The other one wanted it over with.

Could anything be enough for him?  Could anyone love him enough?
     He had a dog, his very own.  The dog was waiting.

He wouldn't find out unless he asked.  But if he did, would anything be left to hope?  But if he didn't how much longer could he wait?  Is it better to not know and pretend?  Or better to know and quit.
     The dog was pawing, readying.

(#1)

# The Mermaid

*Rebecca Brown*

She wanted to be what she was not
she tore apart a part of her
she made herself not speak
she wanted - oh if only! -
who could love her

she made herself breathe differently
we do not breathe the same
some breathe in water, some in air

      **fish:** *a limbless cold-blooded vertebrate animal*
*with gills and fins and living wholly in water.*
                  --*New Oxford American Dictionary*

she wasn't that
she wasn't half
oh what could she be now

sometimes she can't tell things apart
things don't make sense sometimes

she wanted to be remade anew
she made her fish nor fowl
she gasped and gulped and tried to hold
can someone be what she is not
or hold what can't be held
could someone love her

\*

One time from far away she'd seen a prince.  She saw him on a
beach or throne or horse or somewhere she could not recall.  He'd
waved to her she thought but had or had she not waved back?  She
wanted to see him again or once or in the flesh forever.  But soon
she couldn't tell what had been seen or only hoped.  Was she a fool
to hope?  For who oh who oh could he ever love her?

Her mouth hurt with the want of him, his body and his blood.
She hurt with hope and was afraid.  Would hope now be the death of
her or life?

She waited on a rock.  Her mouth was dry.  The sun and waiting
dried and burned and turned her like a leaf.

She couldn't breathe in or out of it
could neither speak nor swim nor cry
was neither fish nor fowl nor girl
nor body blood nor he

She flopped like a fish who couldn't flop.  The sea washed up.  The
sea rolled back.  Some junk was on the beach.  Though papery like
a leaf it oddly stank.  A part of it was torn apart.

Oddly, he gave it a burial.

\*

*I believe this is something.*

(cover)

# Notes on Contributors

**Breka Blakeslee** is a co-editor of Letter [r] Press, a collectively run micropress that publishes the journal *Small Po[r]tions*. Recent work appeared as part of P*oems for a Street Corner,* a street art exhibition for the  Art of the City Street Fest in Seattle.

**Rebecca Brown** is an author, artist, curator, performer and teacher. Her 12 books, published in the US and abroad, include, most recently, *American Romances* (City Lights, 2009), winner of the Publishing Triangle Award.  Other titles include: *The End of Youth, The Dogs: A Modern Bestiary, Annie Oakley's Girl* and *The Terrible Girls*, all with City Lights, *The Gifts of the Body* (HarperCollins) and *Woman in Ill Fitting Wig*, a collaboration with painter Nancy Kiefer. Brown's nonfiction book, *Excerpts from a Family Medical Dictionary*, was published by Granta Books, (UK) and University of Wisconsin Press (USA) and Asahi Shimbun, Japan.

Her altered texts and installations have appeared in museums and galleries in the US and Canada including The Frye Art Museum (Seattle), The Hedreen Gallery (Seattle University), the Poetry Center at the University of Arizona (Tucson) and The Simon Fraser Gallery (Vancouver, BC). Her one-woman performance piece,

"MONSTROUS," which looks at Frankenstein (the novel and the movie) through a quirky lens of literary, feminist, queer and scientific history, autobiography, fantasy, horror and pasta, premiered at Northwest Film Forum in December, 2013. She curated the exhibit "Devotion" at the Hedreen Art Gallery at Seattle University campus and "Breathing the Water," a 3-week, city-wide, multi-venue cultural festival in celebration of the work of poet Denise Levertov in 2015

**Jim Goar** is the author of *The Dustbowl* (Shearsman Books, 2014), *The Louisiana Purchase* (Rose Metal Press, 2011), *Seoul Bus Poems* (Reality Street, 2010), and the chapbook *Whole Milk* (Effing Press, 2006). He lives in Tucson, Arizona.

**Paul Green's** poetry collection *The Gestaltbunker* was published by Shearsman Books in 2012 and a new collection *Shadow Times* is in preparation. His plays include: *The Dream Laboratory* (CBC Canada); *Ritual of the Stifling Air* (BBC Radio 3); *The Voice Collection* (RTE Ireland); *The Mouthpiece* (Resonance FM London); *Terminal Poet* (New Theatre Works Hereford) and *Babalon* ( Travesty Theatre London ) - a collection is due shortly. His fiction includes the novels *The Qliphoth* (Libros Libertad 2007) and *Beneath the Pleasure Zones* (Mandrake of Oxford 2014). He enjoys collaborations with artists using both traditional and electronic media, as well as musicians. His audio work can be found on www.culturecourt.com along with various essays and articles. He lives in Hastings, a small coastal town in the UK.

**Jeff Hilson's** publications include *stretchers* (2006, Reality Street), *The Reality Street Book of Sonnets* (ed.) (2008, Reality Street), *Bird bird* (2009, Landfill) and *In The Assarts* (2010, Veer Books). He is presently working concurrently, sometimes confusingly, on two poem-sequences sections of which have appeared among other places in *Fence, Zone, Molly Bloom, Open Letter, English, VLAK, para-text, Cambridge Literary Review* and as very attractive broadsides from Crater Press. A pamphlet called "A Barry Bendy Poem" came out in the summer of 2015 from Oystercatcher Press. He teaches Creative Writing at the University of Roehampton, London, and runs the reading series Xing the Line.

**Peter Hughes** is a poet and the founding editor of Oystercatcher Press. His *Selected Poems* was published by Shearsman in 2013 along with *'An intuition of the particular': some essays on the poetry of Peter Hughes*, edited by Ian Brinton. 2013 also saw the publication of *Allotment Architecture* by Reality Street, which also published Peter's versions of the complete sonnets of Petrarch under the title *Quite Frankly* in 2015. The first part of his Cavalcanti project is available from Equipage. The complete *Cavalcanty* will be out from Carcanet in 2017.

**Burt Kimmelman's** eighth collection of poetry, *Gradually the World: New and Selected Poems, 1983 – 2013* (BlazeVOX), appeared in 2013. A new collection, *Abandoned Angel* (Marsh Hawk Press), is due out in 2016. His poems have been featured on National Public Radio and are often anthologized, and he has been interviewed both in print and online. He teaches literary and cultural studies at New Jersey Institute of Technology, and has published a number of critical books and more than a hundred articles on literature and other matters. More information about him and samples of his work can be found at BurtKimmelman.com.

**Sarah Mangold** is the author of *Electrical Theories of Femininity* (Black Radish Books), and *Household Mechanics* (New Issues), selected by C.D. Wright for the New Issues Poetry Prize. From 2002-2009 she edited *Bird Dog*, a journal of innovative writing and art. She is the recipient of a 2013 NEA Poetry Fellowship and lives in Edmonds, WA.

**Brian Marley** is searching high and low for the right words.

An English Professor at Central Washington University, **Terry Martin** is the recipient of CWU's Distinguished Professor Teaching Award and the CASE/Carnegie U.S. Professor of the Year Award. Her poems, essays, and articles have appeared in hundreds of publications and she has edited books, journals and anthologies. Her first book of poems, *Wishboats*, won the Judges' Choice Award at Seattle's Bumbershoot Book Fair in 2000; her second book, *The Secret Language of Women*, was published in 2006. Her most recent book of poems, *The Light You Find*, was published by Blue Begonia

Press in 2014. She lives with her family in Yakima, Washington, "The Fruit Bowl of the Nation."

**Andrew Mossin** has published poetry, creative non-fiction and scholarship in *The Iowa Review, Conjunctions, Talisman, Hambone, Callaloo,* and *Contemporary Literature*, among others. His books include two full-length collections of poetry, *The Epochal Body* and *The Veil* (both from Singing Horse Press) and a book of scholarly essays, *Male Subjectivity and Poetic Form in "New American" Poetry* (Palgrave). He is an Assistant Professor in the Intellectual Heritage Program at Temple University.

**Jed Myers** lives in Seattle. Two of his poetry collections, *The Nameless* (Finishing Line Press) and *Watching the Perseids* (winner of the 2013 Sacramento Poetry Center Book Award), are 2014 publications. His work has received Southern Indiana Review's Editors' Award, the Literal Latte Poetry Award, a Pushcart nomination, and, in the UK, a Forward Prize nomination. His poems have appeared or are forthcoming in *I-70 Review, Prairie Schooner, Painted Bride Quarterly, Crab Orchard Review, Nimrod, Lyre Lyre*, and elsewhere.

**Lance Olsen** is author of more than 20 books of and about innovative fiction, including, most recently, the novel *Theories of Forgetting*, the short story collection *How to Unfeel the Dead*, and the trash diary *[[ there. ]]*. He teaches at the University of Utah.

**Marthe Reed** is the author of five books: *Nights Reading* (Lavender Ink 2014), *Pleth*, a collaboration with j hastain (Unlikely Books 2013), *(em)bodied bliss* (Moria Books 2013), *Gaze* (Black Radish Books 2010) and *Tender Box, A Wunderkammer* (Lavender Ink 2007). She has published chapbooks as part of the Dusie Kollektiv, as well as with above/ground press and Shirt Pocket Press. Her collaborative chapbook *thrown*, text by j hastain with Reed's collages, won the 2013 Smoking Glue Gun contest and will appear in 2015. She is co-publisher and managing editor for Black Radish Books and publisher of Nous-zōt Press chapbooks.

**Judith Skillman's** new collection is *House of Burnt Offerings* from Pleasure Boat Studio. Her work has appeared in *Tampa Review, Prairie Schooner, FIELD, The Iowa Review, Poetry, The Southern Review, Midwest Quarterly Review, Seneca Review, New Poets of the American West*, and other journals and anthologies. Skillman is the recipient of grants from the Academy of American Poets, Washington State Arts Commission, The Centrum Foundation, and other organizations. She has taught in the field of humanities for twenty-five years, and has collaboratively translated poems from Italian, Portuguese, and French. Visit www.judithskillman.com

**Philip Terry** is currently Director of the Centre for Creative Writing at the University of Essex. Among his books are the lipogrammatic novel *The Book of Bachelors*, the edited story collection *Ovid Metamorphosed*, a translation of Raymond Queneau's last book of poems *Elementary Morality*, and the poetry volumes *Oulipoems, Oulipoems 2, Shakespeare's Sonnets,* and *Advanced Immorality*. His novel *tapestry* was shortlisted for the 2013 Goldsmith's Prize. *Dante's Inferno*, which relocates Dante's action to current day Essex, was published in 2014, as well as a translation of Georges Perec's *I Remember*.

**Scott Thurston's** most recent book is *Figure Detached Figure Impermanent* (Oystercatcher, 2014). He co-organises The Other Room reading series in Manchester and co-edits the *Journal of British and Irish Innovative Poetry*. Scott lectures at the University of Salford and has published widely on innovative poetry, including a book of interviews entitled *Talking Poetics* (Shearsman, 2011). See his pages at www.archiveofthenow.com.

**Carol Watts** lives in London, where she directs the Contemporary Poetics Research Centre at Birkbeck College. Her poetry includes the collections *many weathers wildly comes* (Spiralbound/Susakpress 2015), *Sundog* (Veer Books, 2013), *Occasionals* (Reality Street Editions, 2011), and *Wrack* (Reality Street Editions, 2007), and the artist's book of prose chronicles *alphabetise* (2005). Her chapbooks include the series *When blue light falls* (Oystercatcher, 2008, 2010, 2012), *this is red* (Torque Press, 2009) and the sonnet sequences *Mother Blake* (2012) and *brass, running* (2006), both with

Equipage. She often works collaboratively, most recently with George Szirtes on an exchange called *56*. She is currently developing a project for live performance and vinyl called T.R.E.E. with the sound artist Will Montgomery, made from creaking trees and rare earths.

# Out in 2015 from REALITY STREET

**OUT OF EVERYWHERE 2**
**Edited by Emily Critchley**
In 1996 Reality Street published Maggie O'Sullivan's anthology of innovative writing by women, *Out of Everywhere*. Nearly 20 years later, here is the sequel...

**Peter Hughes:**
**QUITE FRANKLY**
**After Petrarch's Sonnets**
Versions of all 317 of Petrarch's sonnets, often departing from the originals in radical and startling ways.

**Lou Rowan:**
**ALPHABET OF LOVE SERIAL**
All you need to know about relationships, from A-Z, in 20 stories, by the editor of *Golden Handcuffs Review*.

*Previously ...* Reality Street has published books by Allen Fisher, Barbara Guest, Fanny Howe, David Miller, Maggie O'Sullivan, Denise Riley, Lisa Robertson and these recent selected highlights:

**Bill Griffiths: COLLECTED POEMS & SEQUENCES (1981-91)** and **COLLECTED EARLIER POEMS(1966-80)**
We're publishing all of this late, great British poet's work. These are the first two volumes.

**Ken Edwards:**
**DOWN WITH BEAUTY**
Linked dialogues, dramatic monologues and short fictions exploring exile, war, paranoia, music and nothingness. Includes *Nostalgia for Unknown Cities*, previously published separately.

**Andrea Brady:**
**CUT FROM THE RUSHES**
Philadelphia-born Andrea Brady is one of the most significant poets writing in Britain today. This is her fifth book and her first for Reality Street.

**Philip Terry: TAPESTRY**
Combining magic realism and Oulipian techniques, this re-telling of the 1066 story, inspired by marginal images in the Bayeux Tapestry, was shortlisted for the inaugural Goldsmith's Prize for innovative fiction.

**Richard Makin:**
**DWELLING**
Serialised monthly online (in the best Dickens tradition) over 2006-09, this massive work of "non-generic prose" (novel or art installation?) finally reaches print.

**Paul Griffiths:**
**LET ME TELL YOU**
A novel by this noted musicologist narrated entirely in the 500-word vocabulary Ophelia is allocated in *Hamlet*. "A beautiful and enthralling work" (Harry Mathews)

*You can order all books from our website or from your favourite online or offline retailer. Please visit for up to date news and to go on the mailing list.*

## www.realitystreet.co.uk

www.ingramcontent.com/pod-product-compliance
Lightning Source LLC
Chambersburg PA
CBHW071314200626
46813CB00015B/2190